AGENT of Change

Girl Scouts of the USA

JUNIOR WRITING CIRCLE: Jana Martin, Ann Redpath, Kelli Martin, Laura Tuchman
ILLUSTRATED by Christine Norrie
DESIGNED by Parham Santana

©2008 by Girl Scouts of the USA

First published in 2008 by Girl Scouts of the USA
420 Fifth Avenue, New York, NY 10018-2798
www.girlscouts.org

ISBN: 978-0-88441-713-2

Printed in Italy

4 5 6 7 8 9/16 15 14 13 12 11 10 09 08

Page 18: MPI/Hulton Archive/Getty Images; Page 19: Time Life Pictures/Time & Life Pictures/Getty Images; Page 19: Time Life
Pictures/Time & Life Pictures/Getty Images; Page 19: Alexander Sibaja/Getty Images Entertainment/Getty Images; Page 20: Amy
Graves/WireImage/Getty Images; Page 20: Chad Buchanan/Getty Images Entertainment/Getty Images; Page 21: Andrew Redington/
Getty Images Sport/Getty Images; Page 21: Mark Bowen/Scripps National Spelling Bee; Page 22: MacKenzie Clare Photo courtesy
of Kennedy Krieger Institute; Page 27: Anne Frank Fonds - Basel/Anne Frank House/Hulton Archive/Getty Images; Page 27: Kevin
Scanlon/Getty Images Entertainment/Getty Images.

Fist-to-Five Consensus-Building adapted from: Fletcher, A. (2002). *FireStarter Youth Power Curriculum: Participant Guidebook*. Olympia,
Wash.: Freechild Project.

CONTENTS

Building Circles, from the INSIDE OUT

Welcome

to this journey

where you'll discover your powerful selves.

Not magical power. Real power.

The power you now have.

And not just your individual power

but the amazing power that builds

when you join with your circle

of sister Girl Scouts.

Girl Scout Juniors all across the globe

are making their communities better

by being agents of change.

Who's an agent of change?

A person who discovers

how to use the "power of one"

and the "power of team"

to create the "power of community"

that improves the world.

Let the journey begin!

THE JOURNEY:
What It's All About

Power *isn't* about people who:

- Start everything
- Tell others what to do
- Give speeches

Power *is* the way you act in everyday amazing ways:

- When your little brother asks you to play "horse" for the 89th time—and you do it with a smile. That's power.

- When you notice that the new kid at school sits alone at lunch—and you do something about it. That's power.

- When you figure out how to be part of a team. That's power.

- When you solve problems—your own and the world's. That's power.

→ **POWER** IS SOMETHING YOU CAN SHOW EVERY DAY.

Think About It!

How have you shown your power lately? At home? At school? In your community?

POWERFUL AWARDS

On this journey, you have the opportunity to earn three Girl Scout awards that identify you as a leader: the Power of One Award, the Power of Team Award, and the Power of Community Award. As you travel through this journey, use the nifty Journey Power Award Tracker on the next page to keep track of what you've earned.

Earning these awards means you worked as a team to identify real needs and find real solutions with other leaders like yourself. So treasure these awards. They'll remind you of the Big Ideas you explored on this journey to becoming a girl who changes the world.

Ever wondered how the whole tradition of Girl Scouts earning and awarding badges got started? Juliette Gordon Low once said, "Badges are symbols of things you have learned and have done as a Girl Scout; they stand for that knowledge and for the things you are good at doing and are eager to share with others."

Throughout this book, these buttons will tell you what power you're focused on:

You're in the "you" zone—the Power of One. It's all about you and your power.

You're making the teamwork happen—that's the Power of Team.

You're carrying the action to the world—that's the Power of Community.

"Moxie" means energy, pep, courage, determination, know-how, and expertise—sometimes all rolled into one. As an agent of change, you've got moxie within you. When you gather with others and "moxie up the team," you gather all your collective moxie into one powerful force. You're powering up the team to the max!

7

Journey Power

I DID IT!

ACTION	DATE	REFLECTIONS
The Power of One		
Discover my own powers in a "power log."		
Discover a heroine, past or present.		
Discover how heroines link to the Girl Scout Law.		

Award Tracker

I DID IT!

ACTION	DATE	REFLECTIONS

The Power of Team

Connect with your Girl Scout crew and create a "supergirl" story, comic, or TV script in which the characters take one small situation they care about and strive for a long-lasting community change.

Make a team decision for a Take Action Project and write your Team Hopes.

The Power of Community

Take action on your plan! Get your community involved so that your project can spiral out and change the world.

Reflect on what you accomplished.

> **"** I say, if it's going to be done, let's do it. Let's not put it in the hands of fate. Let's not put it in the hands of someone who doesn't know me. I know me best. **"**
>
> — **Anita Baker,** *Grammy-winning singer-songwriter*

The Power of One

Discover—Yourself!

Ever done something you were proud of? Aced a homework assignment? Pitched in on a family project? Let a worried friend talk your ear off? Made mud pies with your little brother? Or just dealt with crazy stuff?

It takes strength, skill, know-how, patience, and all sorts of qualities to do something you can be proud of.

Everyone, famous or ordinary, has a special blend of qualities. Good at math. Smart with Spanish. Sports whiz. Rock drummer. Artist. The list is endless! And you use these qualities all the time, even when just walking or talking or thinking. You've got the goods to do good!

Think About It!

What do you think about your powers and strengths?

Why are they important?

How do your powers or strengths reflect the values of the Girl Scout Law?

Which value of the Law means the most to you?

YOUR POWER MAKES YOU YOU

me to the MAX

{ Often we're best at what we're interested in. We can spend hours on something we like and not even realize it! What do you like to do? Bet you can do it for a looooong time. Your interests are part of what makes you *you*.

TOP CHEF?

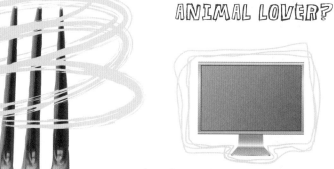

ANIMAL LOVER?

NATURE LOVER?

LIKE LEARNING NEW THINGS?

LOVE TO DANCE?

To be a **good leader**, one thing is certain: You have to discover yourself:
- Your interests
- Your skills
- Your strengths
- Your passions
- YOUR POWERS!

WHAT MAKES ME ME? OR, I'M BEING FRAMED!

SO HOW WOULD YOU DESCRIBE YOU? Paste a photo or drawing of yourself in the center of the frame. Draw lines to connect yourself to the skills and strengths that are YOU. Add your own descriptions of your powers!

THINKER   good listener   ENERGETIC

QUIET

FAST RUNNER

STRONG

considerate

ARTSY OPTION: If you're a collage queen, cut loose with this one! Add photos or illustrations of who and what matter to you. Maybe draw lines from the descriptive words to the pictures.

CONFIDENT

funny

me!

BRAVE

talkative   IMAGINATIVE   GREAT COOK

YOUR DAILY POWER:
SHOUT IT OUT!

Doing just about anything takes a whole lot of skills. And skills are powers. So think about a typical day in your life. How many things do you do that you don't even think about?

me
to the MAX

DID YOU...

- make someone in your family happy by _____

- teach someone how to _____

- help someone get better at _____

- comfort a friend by _____

- _____ even though everyone else was

_____

- learn _____ at school, so that at home you could _____

- make a _____ for yourself or someone else

Use the Power Log on the next page to list all the powers *you* use in just one day. The Power Log is a Power of One Award experience. After you complete your log, fill in your Journey Power Award Tracker on page 8.

Look out, loggers! I'll show you how to power through a day!

x

POWER LOG

Keep a power log for one full day. Keep track in any way you like. Share it with others!

Morning

Afternoon

Evening

Pool Your Powers

Next time you're hanging out with friends, why not talk about everything you did that day? Share your **personal power** list. Ask your friends what's on their list. Compare your powers. You may discover that you're a circle of SUPERGIRLS.

The Good News

me to the MAX

These days, you can pursue your dreams, no matter how far they reach. You can head a company, run a team, be a leader in your community, run for president, drive a bus, design a supersonic plane, go to the moon or beyond, start a record label, play the organ or the drums or the flute or the bongos, design fabulous clothing, make 25-story cakes, build bridges, try to solve world hunger, save the polar bears. You name it, you can do it!

And if anyone's surprised? Tell them lots of women have done amazing things. The world just doesn't always hear about them.

All this power! I need some perspective. And some good stories! Give me some herstory— right now!

TELL HER STORY! It's time to take back history! Find one woman or girl from the past and check out her life. What did she do? How? Share what you uncover. To get you started, look at the *Herstory* bios on the following pages. See if you are interested in any of them. Or pick a woman or girl who is doing it all right now. Check into her world. Share it!

LOOKING BACK AT
HERSTORY

Did you know . . .

- Until about 500 years ago, women were rarely credited for their inventions, cooking, art, or writing.

- Few of women's courageous contributions to society were recognized.

- Except in the case of a few members of royalty, the works left behind were simply labeled "Unidentified" or "Anonymous."

- It didn't matter how hard they tried or how big they dreamed—early women were often forgotten in the pages of history.

WOMEN
FROM THE PAGES OF *HERSTORY*

The Ultimate Truth-Teller: Sojourner Truth (1797-1883)

Isabella Baumfree changed her name to what was true about herself. "Sojourner" means someone who travels, and you already know what "truth" means! She changed her name after she freed herself from slavery. She then traveled the country, speaking the truth about the cruel treatment she and her family received as slaves, and called for an end to slavery. She also spoke about women needing the same rights as men—like the right to buy and own a home. Sojourner's gift to us: showing what it means to speak out for what we believe in.

Milla the Schoolmaster: Milla Granson (1816-circa 1870)

Milla Granson, also known as Lily Ann Granderson, was one of America's most important educators. Born enslaved and forbidden to read and write, she still learned to do both—from her slave-owner's children. And guess how she put her new knowledge to use? By organizing a secret school where classes were held late at night so slave children could sneak out and attend. For more than seven years, she helped educate hundreds of slaves in Mississippi and other states. What Granson stood for: risks worth taking and education for all.

Proud and Persistent: Maria Stewart (1803-1879)

In the early 1830s, Maria Stewart became the first black public speaker. In her first speech, she urged people to work to stop slavery and to be proud of their race, culture, and heritage. Her speeches upset a lot of people—she even had to stop speaking publicly in order to guarantee her safety. But she found other ways to instill pride in people and make a living—she founded schools in Washington and Baltimore, taught in church groups, and assisted at hospitals. What do we learn from Stewart? Pride in work and in freedom.

Angel of Moses: Harriet Tubman (1820-1913)

People called Harriet Tubman "Moses" for the heroic trips she made leading people from slavery in the South to freedom in the North along the Underground Railroad. She proudly stated that she "never lost a single passenger" on that vast network of safe houses. Harriet knew it was risky making those trips—19 in all! But she saved more than 300 women, men, and children from slavery—including her parents and brothers. Her work was so successful that her enemies put out a reward of $40,000 (equal to $1,000,000 today!) for Harriet to be stopped. Yet she was never caught. Even after slavery ended, Harriet kept speaking for freedom, inspiring both black and white audiences. During the Civil War, she worked as a scout and spy, and became the first woman to command an armed military raid, which liberated more than 700 slaves. What Harriet taught us: how to strive to be a life saver and life protector—over and over and over again, any way we can.

Queen of the Farm: Dolores Huerta (born 1930)

A Girl Scout just like you, Dolores Huerta became known for fighting for the rights of agricultural workers. Her mother, a businesswoman, allowed farm worker families to stay for free in her 70-room hotel. As an adult working with community service organizations, Huerta lobbied for public assistance programs for farm workers and their families. She received many awards for her work serving farm workers, Latinos, immigrants, and youth. Her contribution: equal rights on the farms that give this rainbow nation its food.

WHO'S IN THE PAGES OF YOUR FAMILY'S HERSTORY?

_____

_____

_____

_____

_____

_____

_____

Dream Team
Trading Cards

Athlete, actress, senator, designer, writer, activist, architect, doctor, zookeeper, chef, inventor— **women lead with their powers!**

America Ferrera, actor

Leader in field:
This Los Angeleno, who traces her roots to Honduras, has won awards for playing the lead in the hit TV show "Ugly Betty." Acting since age 11.

Leader in world:
She speaks out for Latinas and against stereotypes.

Quotable:
Ferrera has been known to say that it's so reassuring to have a woman heroine who triumphs with more than just what she has on the outside!

Dakota Fanning, actor

Leader in field:
Acting alongside some of the biggest names in Hollywood, she has won the respect of the acting community for her professionalism. Acting since age 5.

Leader in world:
An active Girl Scout, she works with Starlight Starbright Children's Foundation, helping chronically ill kids, and the American Red Cross.

Quotable:
"It doesn't matter what car you drive and what apartment or house you live in, or even what you look like on the outside. It just matters what your heart looks like."

Serena and Venus Williams, athletes

Leaders in field:
The dynamic duo of tennis. These two sisters began winning tournaments at age 10. Venus: four-time Wimbledon women's champ, fastest serve ever recorded by a female player (128.8 miles an hour!). Serena: has won nearly everything in women's tennis, a self-described perfectionist; also known for toughness, spirit, and style. Both: fought injuries, came back champs.

Leader in world:
Venus helped change the system of unequal pay for female and male tennis players. Serena organizes tennis matches for urban kids.

Quotable:
"Somewhere in the world, a little girl is dreaming of holding a giant trophy in her hands and being viewed as an equal to boys who have similar dreams." —Venus

Katherine "Kerry" Close, National Spelling Bee champion

Leader in field:
At 13, Kerry won the 2006 Scripps National Spelling Bee by spelling "Ursprache," which means "protolanguage" (ur = original + sprache = language). This New Jersey girl was first to win the Bee on prime-time TV—talk about pressure!

Leader in world:
As a Bee champ, Kerry's been an inspiration to thousands to study hard. Her chosen career: journalism.

Quotable:
"U-r-s-p-r-a-c-h-e."

MacKenzie Clare, living-with-disabilities educator

Leader in world:
Skier, skater, and active Girl Scout, MacKenzie was only 10 when everything she loved to do stopped. A car accident paralyzed her from the chest down; she and her parents were in the hospital for three months. As she learned to manage wheelchair living, MacKenzie recognized the help that so many people had given her. Her response? Accept her situation, teach others about living with a disability, and, along the way, become an inspiration to all.

Quotable:
"It just doesn't seem fair that a child should have to deal with this, but then again . . . no one should!!"

Amy Poe, community organizer

Leader in world:
Amy breaks down language barriers. Traveling in Mexico, she saw how tough it was to live in a culture that spoke a language she didn't know. So she used her Girl Scout Gold Award project to help Spanish speakers back in Georgia. Her Hispanic directory gives access to vital services and information—in Spanish.

Quotable:
"I learned that I can accomplish a large task one step at a time."

Dream On: Use these cards to start
your own Dream Team collection! Add more! Add anyone you admire! Add your friends! Add YOURSELF.

(Your Name Here)

Leader in field:
(Describe yourself!)
_ _ _ _ _ _ _ _ _ _ _ _ _ _ _
_ _ _ _ _ _ _ _ _ _ _ _ _ _ _
_ _ _ _ _ _ _ _ _ _ _ _ _ _ _
_ _ _ _ _ _ _ _ _ _ _ _ _ _ _

Leader in world:
(Past, present, and future!)
_ _ _ _ _ _ _ _ _ _ _ _ _ _ _
_ _ _ _ _ _ _ _ _ _ _ _ _ _ _
_ _ _ _ _ _ _ _ _ _ _ _ _ _ _

Quotable:
(What would you like people to know?)
_ _ _ _ _ _ _ _ _ _ _ _ _ _ _
_ _ _ _ _ _ _ _ _ _ _ _ _ _ _
_ _ _ _ _ _ _ _ _ _ _ _ _ _ _

Remember to fill in your Journey Power Award Tracker on page 8.

to the MAX

One Way to Share Your *Her*story

Pick one or two role models from history or the present. Turn them into Dream Team trading cards like the ones on the previous pages.

THE REAL ME

Ever want to say crazy things about yourself and see if your friends believe you? Ever want to just SPILL IT and admit something you usually hide—some deep truth? Ever want to describe yourself in a way you wish you could be?

To be a leader, you have to know yourself. But how well do others know you? Play this game and find out:

Think of something true, something false, and something you wish for. In secret, write each item on a card with the correct "True," "False," or "Wish" labeled on the back. Keep your cards hidden and get out your best poker face. Then gather in a circle with friends. Go around the circle and have each girl say one thing about herself. The rest of you have to decide whether it's true, false, or a wish. Can you fool anyone—or everyone—when it's your turn? This game is a great way to get to know each other!

OPTION: When you're with your friends, try a wishing session. Make your own wish cards by writing down 10 wishes. Share them. Do any of you share the same wish?

I wish I was on a football team.

I wish I could see Africa.

I wish that I lived in a small town instead of a big city.

I wish I could rock out in a band.

I wish I owned a store and could give everything to people who needed it for FREE.

I wish I had a racehorse.

I wish I had arms so long I could slam dunk better than my brother.

> " The pages of the history of the future may hold your names in a high and honored place. Do your part today. "
>
> —Juliette Gordon Low

YOU'RE AT THE END OF THE FIRST LEG OF THE JOURNEY! AND YOU DISCOVERED A GIRL WHO IS A NATURAL-BORN LEADER **} YOU!**

THE POWER OF WORDS

Been seeing some powerful words on this journey?
Here's a mini-glossary for handy reference.

ceremony

A way to mark and celebrate an important event, feeling, or experience in our lives.

change agent

A person who has the intention to cause a change—in society or culture or even in behavior. A change agent looks for better ways to do things; the agent decides on a change and does it.

circle

As a noun, a curved line along which all points are the same distance from the center; a group of people having the same things in common. As a verb, to bring around or gather.

community

A group of people living in the same place (like a neighborhood), people who share a common background or interests (such as park volunteers or Girl Scout group members), or countries with a common history or economic or political interests (like the European nations).

mobilize

To make active or capable of action; to enable a group of individuals to take collective action in pursuit of a common goal or to become active participants in society.

moxie

Energy, pep, courage, determination, know-how, expertise—sometimes all rolled into one!

Add in some of your own power words, too.

WORD POWER! DO THE MATH!

Do you add these or multiply them?

Belief __ friends __ moxie ___ ideas = ingenuity

Ingenuity = cleverness ___ originality

Belief ___ ingenuity = Mega moxie girl power!

Power Skills, Power Words

Circle all the power words you can find in the grid below. Not just words with power in them, but all the skills, qualities, and attributes that a powerful person—an agent of change!—might have. The words are hidden up, down, across, diagonal, even backward.

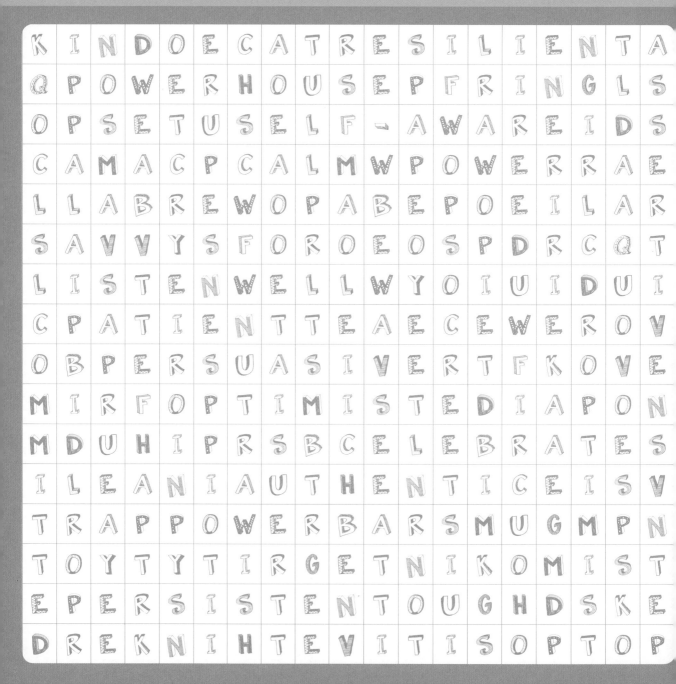

```
K I N D O E C A T R E S I L I E N T A
Q P O W E R H O U S E P F R I N G L S
O P S E T U S E L F - A W A R E I D S
C A M A C P C A L M W P O W E R R A E
L L A B R E W O P A B E P O E I L A R
S A V V Y S F O R O E O S P D R C Q T
L I S T E N W E L L W Y O I U I D U I
C P A T I E N T T E A C E W E R O V
O B P E R S U A S I V E R T F K O V E
M I R F O P T I M I S T E D I A P O N
M D U H I P R S B C E L E B R A T E S
I L E A N I A U T H E N T I C E I S V
T R A P P O W E R B A R S M U G M P N
T O Y T Y T I R G E T N I K O M I S T
E P E R S I S T E N T O U G H D S K E
D R E K N I H T E V I T I S O P T O P
```

REAL GIRLS, REAL MOXIE: STORIES THAT INSPIRE

Anne Frank: A Diary for the World

Anne Frank received a diary for her 13th birthday. She wrote in it from June 1942 to August 1944, while she and her family were in hiding in Amsterdam during World War II. When Anne Frank's father, Otto, returned to Amsterdam as the sole family member to survive the Nazi concentration camps, Miep Gies, his bookkeeper and friend who helped hide the family (and also supplied notebooks to Anne), gave the diary to Mr. Frank.

Anne's diary began as her private thoughts. She wrote about her family and companions and how they lived in hiding in the cramped attic, fearing for their lives. As she wrote, she realized that she wanted to be a writer. Anne died in a concentration camp in 1945 at age 15, but her diary lives on. It has been published in more than 100 languages and continues to inspire readers all over the world.

Marjane Satrapi, Graphic Novel Author

Marjane Satrapi has a way of laughing and surviving in the face of terrible obstacles. In *Persepolis*, a graphic novel that is both personal and political, she tells the story of her youth in Tehran during the Islamic Revolution and the Iranian war with Iraq.

Marjane now lives in France. She loves to talk about writing a graphic novel: "It's like making a movie," she says. "We learn about the world through images all the time. Movies do it with lots of people, but with a graphic novel, you just need yourself and your pen or pencil."

Marjane believes that "there are peaceful ways to solve the world's problems." Telling her story is one of those peaceful ways. In 2007, it was released as an animated feature film.

Who Led the Way for YOU?

Coach? Teacher? Friend? Parent? Write down your favorite leaders.
Talk to your friends about theirs.

_____

_____

_____

A leader can be . . .

Anyone, anywhere.
She may live on the other side of the globe,
  or right next door.
See with perfect vision
  or not see at all.
Run like the wind
  or be a whiz in a wheelchair.
Be very old
  or very young.
Be in the White House
  or in 4th or 5th grade.
YOU.

A leader:

Cares enough to want to do something.

Believes the job will get done.

Inspires others to do their best.

Appreciates working with others.

Makes others feel great about their work.

Listens and takes advice.

Strives for group success.

Think About It!

Why is listening well a sign of a good leader?

POWERFUL WORDS

In comic books, they're called **superheroes**. In stories, they're called heroes and heroines. What other words describe leaders? Make up your own word!

_____

_____

_____

*Megasuperultrasmartypants
teacherfrom3rdgrade*

28

REAL POWERS, REAL GIRL SCOUTS

me to the MAX

The Girl Scout Law Meets the "Heroines" in Me

In real life, it takes real people to tackle real issues. You don't need to wear a superhero's cape to grab a real-world situation and save the day! You just need to be YOU.

When you act in any of the ways that the Girl Scout Law suggests, how are you acting heroically and powerfully? Get together with your sister Girl Scouts and see what they say. Pick your favorite value of the Law and lead the way!

When I act in an honest way, I am showing

_____

And for the other key qualities, what would you say?

Fair _____   Strong _____

Friendly _____   Responsible _____

Helpful _____   Respectful _____

Considerate _____   Use resources wisely _____

Caring _____   A sister to every Girl Scout _____

Courageous _____   _____

The Real Powers, Real Girl Scouts activity is the final step to earning your **Power of One Award.** The activity strengthens your understanding of how the Girl Scout Law builds the kind of powers real-life heroines need.

You're About to Earn Your First Award Don't Forget to Celebrate!

Celebrations are important. So are ceremonies. They call us away from the everyday. They take a special accomplishment, feeling, or life event and make a big way of saying, "This is worth remembering." We may not use those exact words, but we "say it" by singing, dancing, eating special foods, telling certain stories.

Getting Together in Circles

Ceremonies have been around for a long time—and so have circles. In fact, people have been getting together in circles to celebrate something special in their lives for thousands of years.

Circles are important in Girl Scout ceremonies—from Friendship Circles and squeezes to just standing around in a circle to meet and talk. Circles have no beginning and no ending. They bring people together—face-to-face.

So join with your sister Girl Scouts and plan some ceremonies for this journey. Or split into pairs and take turns planning ceremonies (and being the emcee). It's one more way to be a leader.

Using Symbols in Your Ceremonies

Girl Scouting has lots of symbols—the friendship squeeze, the handshake, the sign. Signs and symbols can make your ceremony feel richer, more special. Here are some other symbols and what they represent:

CANDLE OR FLASHLIGHT	the light within each person
STRING/ROPE	the thread that unites everyone
BRANCH	peace
FLAG	official banner
PEBBLE	nature

What symbols do you like—from Girl Scouting and from life?

PACK SOME FUN INTO YOUR CEREMONIES

Ceremonies are meant to be meaningful, but they don't have to be serious. They might be solemn—if you are honoring someone or setting aside quiet time to think and reflect. Mostly, though, your ceremonies should be *your* ceremonies. And they should be fun. You can do a skit, sing a song, dance, cheer or chant, or simply talk. Aim to create a mood. Above all, be simple, be yourselves, and enjoy your ceremonies.

A ceremony can provide a great energy boost. Throughout the journey, you'll see some suggestions to get you thinking about your awards ceremonies. Here's one for your Power of One Award, which you're probably ready to earn right about now:

In a circle, cross arms for a friendship squeeze. Go around the circle and say one thing that you can imagine Juliette Gordon Low congratulating your group for having just done.

Remember to fill in your Journey Power Award Tracker on page 8!

I say, par-teeee! I love a good celebration. And I know just what to wear.

I've been weaving my web solo for so long. But I would so love a team. There's beauty in teamwork—and power, too.

" When spider webs unite, they can tie up a lion."

— Ethiopian proverb

The Power of Team

GREAT LEADERS AND GREAT TEAMS

Moxie up the team

What makes a great team? Great leaders! When each person takes a lead and does her part. When everyone on the team cares about meeting the goals.

Talk with your friends about what's most important for a team. Here's a start: Teams are made of up leaders. Teams of leaders don't hesitate to make a decision—to do something. They step up to the plate and take action.

But team leaders don't do it all themselves. They reach out to more people. They talk. They listen. They grow and strengthen their team!

When it comes to getting something done, there's nothing stronger than a group. When you team together, you can score a goal for the globe.

Now, talk with your friends about what makes a bad team. How many bad qualities did you come up with?

Every negative has an opposite, so try to find the positive! Make a list of words that describe how people act in a great team. Here are a few to get you started:

> listen well
>
> energetic
>
> confident

Go, Team!

What if, whenever you faced a difficult situation, issue, or challenge, you could tackle it with a team? When you add your special strengths and skills to your friends' strengths and skills, you have a whole new set of ideas, hands, and tools to work with!

So team up, lead on, and have fun! It's time to **moxie up the team**.

WHAT MAKES A GOOD LEADER?

Circle the qualities you want the leaders on your team to have so your team really rocks. Add in any other qualities you can think of.

- Wants to help (sticks her neck out to do it!)
- Sees problems as things to fix (not complain about)
- Sees issues as things to deal with (not run from)
- Wants to work with others
- Says, "Together, we can do it!" (and you believe her)
- Makes others feel valued (thanks for the props, pal!)
- Is a good communicator (totally clear)
- Takes the time (even if it's a loooong time)
- Listens to others (hey, I hear you!)
- Takes teammates' advice (always a good idea)
- Is creative (thinks outside the box)
- Inspires confidence (follow me, I'm right with you)
- Keeps smiling (no worries)
- Is _____
- Is _____
- Is _____
- Is _____

ONE TEAM, MANY LEADERS

So now it's pretty clear: Teams often have many leaders—not just one. As in soccer—it's not just the girl who scores who's the leader. Everyone has a lead role: the goalie, the defense, even your parents or little sister cheering on the sideline.

Think About It!

What leadership role do you play on the teams in your life—in Girl Scouts, in your family, in your neighborhood?

Do you see how all this power is spiraling out—like a great big web? First me—well, you!—then the team, and then . . . Where will this web weave next?

OPTION:

When you have a team, you gotta have trust. Want to find out more about trust on your team? Try the game below.

Break into small teams, maybe four or five girls, and have one girl put on a blindfold. That girl then lets the rest of the team lead her around. Want to find out if you can trust your team? Take a turn wearing the blindfold!

You'll see what it's like to:

- be responsible for someone else.
- let someone else guide you.
- learn how to trust each other.

Moxie up the
team

Take it outdoors.

Set up your own obstacle course outdoors with friends. (Just don't make it too hard—no one wants to get hurt.) Grab an adult to keep an eye out and give advice.

Then take some time to reflect.

Whenever you try new challenges with your friends, it's good to take a minute to talk about it afterward: Was it fun to do? Was it hard? Did it get easier? How did it feel to be the follower? How did it feel to be the leader? Would you do it again?

Hey, I wouldn't mind weaving my own webby obstacle course! Nothing builds trust faster than having to trust someone.

BUILDING CONSENSUS

When you have a team, you want all your members working together. When you all agree on what to do, that's called reaching a "consensus." A "con-**whats**-sus?" A con**sens**us . . . because it makes a lot of sense to work as a team if you want to get things done!

When you reach a consensus, does that mean everyone in the group thinks exactly the same? Uh-uh! It means that everyone in the group can support the same decision or agree to live with it. And when different groups have to work together, building consensus is the way important things get done.

How can your girl circle build consensus? Try the "Fist-to-Five" technique! Everybody starts by holding up their tightly closed fists. The speaker states her opinion about what she thinks the group needs to do, and then everyone uses her fingers to do the talking:

- A closed fist means "Complete disagreement."

- A pinky finger extended with other fingers closed means "Need to discuss issue further."

- Two fingers extended means "Still not ready to agree, but let's talk more."

- Three fingers extended means "I can live with it."

- Four fingers extended means "It's a good idea."

- All fingers extended means "It's great—I want to lead this!"

Depending on how many fingers are showing, the group either continues discussing the issue or moves ahead in agreement. Sometimes when you're on a team, it's important for everybody to be totally excited—all fingers up! But sometimes that's not so important and some team members might compromise. Being a team member is all about being in tune with what will really get the whole team moving forward.

Now try "Fist to Five" with some friends. To get you started, here are two things to try to reach a consensus on:

- The best movie for us to see together would be?

- A great game to play to build our team spirit would be?

Think About It!

When you are part of a team, why do you think negotiating a decision is important?

WHO CAN MOBILIZE THE MOXIE?

When you can mobilize the moxie in others as well as in yourself, you're demonstrating leadership, organization skills, and teamwork. It means you and your teammates are becoming heroines in your own lives.

Let's look at some young heroines who truly mobilized the moxie.

THE POWER OF ONE GOOD IDEA

Talia, Disaster-Relief Coordinator

At age 10, Talia was already tired of lemonade stands. "There's got to be another way to help bring relief for the people after Hurricane Katrina," Talia said as she folded up her lemonade table one more time. Then she had a great idea: Halloween was coming, and kids could ask for help for those affected by Hurricane Katrina.

Talia got a local food chain to print 8 million trick-or-treat grocery bags that stated how much the people of New Orleans needed help and support. She appealed to the governor of her state, Iowa. He spread the word to governors' offices around the country.

Talia is the CEO of randomkid.org, a non-profit organization that helps children solve real world problems by tapping into resources and inspiring and mobilizing others. Says Talia, "I learned that you can do anything if you put your mind to it. When it gets hard, just remember all the people you are helping."

DANCING AS AN ACT OF COURAGE

The Iraqi National Folklore Group, Dancers

The 10 young women who are part of this dance group risk their lives with each performance in their own country. Females are forbidden to participate in folk dancing by Islamic rule. One 21-year-old dancer received a bullet in an envelope warning her to leave the group within 48 hours.

When she is onstage, this young woman has said she feels free as a bird. After dancing, she covers her head and the lower part of her face with a scarf and walks proudly through the streets of her hometown. Her dance group, dedicated to keeping alive the country's heritage, continues to perform all over the world.

LEADING THE WAY TO LASTING CHANGE

Haley and Rosie, Community Organizers

When Haley and Rosie learned that an 8-year-old neighbor was killed by his mother's boyfriend, the two friends knew they wanted to help prevent such abuse. They created an awareness campaign in their hometown of Hammond, Wisconsin. First, they researched and found resources through school counselors and the Web. Then they made wristbands, buttons, and bookmarks and distributed them to merchants around town. "We wanted kids to know that they have a right to feel safe physically and emotionally, and that there are ways to get help," said Haley. A Girl Scout, she earned her Silver Award with this project.

Which of these young heroines stands out to you? Why?

Do you know anyone whose moxie you can match?

I love good stories, especially true ones—the kind that just melt my heart. How about a few more? And then maybe a big one—something I can really get tangled up in!

TURNING ACTION INTO GOLD

Some young action-takers turn good community service projects into long-lasting efforts—by making great choices. The following Girl Scouts went on to earn their Girl Scout Gold Awards and the added honor of "Young Women of Distinction" from Girl Scouts of the USA. They offer inspiration to anyone who wants to change the world—today or in the future.

Laura, of Miami, Florida, helped more than 40 children get life-changing operations that their families couldn't possibly pay for on their own. As a volunteer for Operation Smile, she assisted more than 400 families facing serious medical situations. And she didn't stop there. She helped produce educational materials—in several languages!—to teach families about the program.

Two sisters, **Amrita** and **Shrutika**, wanted to end the cycle of poverty in the rural village of Tamil Nadu, India. With support from village elders and the help of sponsors, they improved the quality of education in the village school. And that meant they also way upped the school spirit of village children.

> "There are some things you do alone, but generally speaking, the ones you work on with others are more fun. . . One thing is sure—you want to be proud. . . and feel that you have accomplished something worthwhile."
>
> —Juliette Gordon Low

Word Play

What Makes a Great Leader Also Makes a Great Team!

Write one sentence about what your Girl Scout team has been doing—and use
as many of these words as possible:

Cooperation

Appreciation

Commitment

Enthusiasm

Caring

Dedication

Creativity

Courage

Communication

Confidence

Now, how about a picture story?
Follow the prompts to create a story of what your team is up to.

Scene 1: We've Got a Problem to Solve

Scene 2: We're Finding Resources—Especially People

Scene 3: We Set Our Goals

Scene 4: We Break into Project Teams

Scene 5: We Make a Progress Report

Scene 6: We Think About What We Did, We Talk About It, and We Celebrate!

The Power of Story

Well, we've made it through some pretty awesome powers: Power of One and Power of Team. Now I'm ready to stretch these legs of mine. After all, we can't be agents of change if we don't get out into the community.

As I said at the start of this journey, I'm really into reading—especially stories. How about a powerful story to carry us forward?

Go ahead, read! I'll be weaving my way right by your side.

IT WAS JUST ANOTHER PERFECT SPRING DAY IN THE SMALL TOWN OF GLENVILLE—AN ORDINARY, SUN-SHINY, SOFT BREEZE-BLOWING DAY, LIKE ANY OTHER.

Did you know it takes 535 steps just to walk around the block?

Of course, that's approximate—I mean, it would take you maybe 550 steps, and me 520, probably.

Remember me? I'm Dez. It takes a whole lotta styles to express my girl power.

Like today, when I get all glammed out and mix trendy with classic.

Other days I'm all athletic—or even a little goth!

A girl can't be boxed in, you know!

Wow. How do you *know* how to do *that?*

It runs in the *family.* My mom's a *veterinarian—* remember?

I've been taking *care* of animals since before I could *walk.*

You know how some kids have *stuffed* animals?

I had a stuffed *pink* bunny named *Crash.*

I had *real* ones. And they were hungry.

Whoa, got distracted there. Where was I?

Oh! The skinny on Sun-ah. She's all-out animal-licious!

She knows how to calm 'em, feed 'em, teach 'em.

...but what about you?!

What's your power?

Not "authority" power!

I mean your special mix of strength and skills.

You know, what you're great at— really passionate about!

What makes you *you?*

THERE IS NO SIGN OF THE PUPS' MOTHER.

Now what, Dr. Doolittle?

I'd say it's *time* to find them a *home!*

THE GIRLS SPRING INTO ACTION!

Mom, we've got an *emergency!*

Come on! Fess up!

What's your super-duper power?

While you think about that, I'm out like shout.

So many outfits, so little time!

11

CHAPTER 2: PUPPY POWER!

IT'S FIVE LONG BLOCKS TO SUN-AH'S HOUSE!

Maybe 40! Can you slow down?

Your *arms* are a lot longer than mine.

I'd say we've got about *35 pounds* of pup here, maybe 36.

See? I told you Megan was nutty for numbers!

By the way, you knew I'd change my outfit, right?

Being Dez rocks!

Three and a *quarter* inches each, actually.

But if we *walk* in *sync*, we should be able to compensate and keep the box *steady*.

One-two, left-right—

WORKING TOGETHER, THEY GET THE BOX OF PUPS TO SUN-AH'S HOUSE.

Good thing I'm wearing sneakers.

If you thought I was some fashionista couch potato, girl, were you wrong!

So, how do you keep active?

DR. FAN, SUN-AH'S MOTHER, IS ALREADY AT THE HOUSE — WITH A TON OF SUPPLIES!

If my daughter says it's an emergency, I believe her. She's very convincing.

I knew she was busy, but I wanted her to feel what these puppies were going through.

You went *15.5 miles* in the time it took us to walk five blocks, Dr. Fan!

I told her, "How would you like to be abandoned in a box? You'd miss your family, your friends; you'd be cold, and you wouldn't be able to go anywhere."

IT'S TRUE: SUN-AH HAS A SPECIAL ABILITY TO CONVINCE PEOPLE BY SAYING JUST THE RIGHT THING.

TA all the way!

That's what I call Taking Action.

That Sun-ah is good!

Step into her shoes: What would you have said?

How would you convince an important adult to join in on your pet project?

THE GIRLS HELP DR. FAN CHECK EACH PUP.

You could have just *left* them, hoping someone *else* would help.

I'm *proud* of you girls.

Such *lucky* pups.

MEGAN LEARNS HOW TO HOLD THE PUPS BY SUPPORTING THE HIND LEGS WITH ONE HAND AND THE CHEST WITH THE OTHER.

SHE CAN FEEL EACH PUPPY'S QUICK-BEATING HEART IN THE PALM OF HER HAND.

Instead, you took *charge* of the situation.

You may have *saved* their lives!

We couldn't *leave* them.

It wouldn't have been *right*.

Don't you love how Sun-ah and her mom look so much alike?

And how they both love animals?

What have you inherited from your family? C'mon, there's gotta be something!?

THE GIRLS SOON REALIZE THEY HADN'T QUITE FACTORED EVERYTHING IN WHEN THEY BROUGHT THE PUPS HOME.

So what's your next *move*? These pups are going to get *big* fast.

They *need* to be fed, watered, bathed, housetrained, walked—

and *that's* just for *starters*.

Maybe a time-management system would work.

How *much* time per pup would you *estimate*?

At *least* three hours.

Per *day*, per *pup*.

Yeesh!

When!

Not even I need that much time to get my glam self together!

But no one's *here* all day—Sun-ah, you're in *school*, and your father and I are both at *work*.

You're right. *Hmmm*.

As you can see, puppies need *a lot* of supervision.

We're going to need some *help* figuring this one out!

IT'S TIME TO TAKE ACTION — AGAIN!

How about we call our *Girl Scout group* for an emergency meeting?

And let's make sure *the twins* can get over here right now.

If *anyone* can help us figure this out, *they* can!

DR. FAN IS RIGHT. THEY NEED HELP—FAST!

So cool that the girls care enough to want to do something!

Something that makes a difference in the world.

Say you and your friends found these pups: What would you do?

CHAPTER 4: THE SHELTER NEEDS HELP, TOO

FOR THE NEXT 10 MINUTES, SHE TELLS THE GIRLS ALL THE SHELTER'S DRAMA. . . .

. . . HOW THE SHELTER LOST ITS FUNDING IN THE BUDGET CUTS LAST YEAR, AND SO LOST ITS STAFF, TOO . . .

. . . HOW AN ELDERLY MAN HAD DIED AND LEFT HIS CATS IN HER CARE—14 IN ALL!

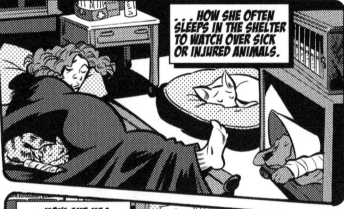

. . . HOW SHE OFTEN SLEEPS IN THE SHELTER TO WATCH OVER SICK OR INJURED ANIMALS.

. . . HOW SHE HAS NO TIME TO GET VOLUNTEERS BECAUSE SHE IS TOO BUSY WATCHING THE ANIMALS . . .

. . . AND HOW ADOPTIONS ARE DOWN, BECAUSE FEW PEOPLE WANT TO VISIT SUCH A RUNDOWN SHELTER.

WITH THE PUPPIES SAFE AT THE SHELTER, THE GIRLS WASTE NO TIME.

AT THEIR EMERGENCY GIRL SCOUT MEETING, THEY GET MRS. LOPEZ, THEIR TROOP GUIDE, TO HELP THEM HOLD A "HELP THE SHELTER" FAIR THE FOLLOWING SATURDAY AFTERNOON AT THEIR SCHOOL.

THEY START WITH MRS. LOPEZ BECAUSE THEY WANT TO GET THEIR WHOLE TROOP INVOLVED, AND THEN THE WHOLE SCHOOL, AND MAYBE EVEN THE WHOLE TOWN.

You know I'm *always* trying to get you girls *involved* in the *community*.

So I'm *proud* of you for wanting to *lead* the way.

Let's see who else we can get involved.

TO THE GIRLS' ASTONISHMENT, IN WALKS THE PRINCIPAL—AND OTHER TEACHERS—AND THE BASKETBALL COACH! IT'S LIKE A GIANT STAFF MEETING!

Go ahead.

You girls are in charge.

Talk about going global! Or should I say viral? Just by asking for help, look how many people are now involved!

If you had a great project like this, what first step would you take to get everybody on board?

THE GIRLS TAKE CARE TO KEEP THEIR PITCH SHORT AND SWEET.

And we figure if we can get our *whole group* involved and our *school*—

then the *town* will follow.

There's only *one* problem.

FOR THE FAIR, THE GIRL SCOUTS PLAN CARNIVAL GAMES WITH PRIZES. BUT FOLKS HAVE TO PAY TO PLAY: PAY WITH THEIR TIME!

TO PLAY A GAME, A PERSON HAS TO "BUY" A TICKET— EACH TICKET COSTS THEM ONE HOUR OF THEIR TIME. THE GIRLS PLAN GAME BOOTHS FOR THE TOWN'S PET STORE OWNERS, TRAINERS, AND VETS.

TOWNSPEOPLE JUST HAVE TO STOP BY THE BOOTHS THEY THINK ARE THE MOST FUN AND "PAY TO PLAY" THERE.

Plus, when people come to *your* booth and *donate* their hour to play a game, they'll split *their* time, spending 30 minutes of that *hour* helping at the *shelter* and 30 minutes on another day *helping* out at *your* business.

In exchange for *participating*, you'll gain a lot of *exposure*.

Sounds *great* to me!

You'll *meet* dozens of pet-owning *families* you'd *love* to have as customers.

THE GIRL SCOUTS ALSO PLAN A "MEET THE ANIMALS" BOOTH WHERE ARDEN LANG CAN INTRODUCE THE TOWN TO ALL THE SHELTER'S DOGS AND CATS—TO MAYBE GET SOME ADOPTED.

FOR THE PUPPIES, THEY PLAN A "PET THE PUPS FOR GOOD LUCK!" BOOTH.

Way to go, Sun-ah! She's the Convincing Queen!

She showed how the trainer could benefit—and do some good for the shelter, too.

Have you ever had to convince someone to join a project you were passionate about?

AT SCHOOL, THE GIRLS MARCH INTO THE ART CLASS AND GET FIVE VOLUNTEERS TO FORM A DECORATING COMMITTEE.

THEY GO TO THE CARPENTRY CLASS AND GET FIVE MORE VOLUNTEERS TO BUILD THE BOOTHS.

Dig the teamwork—and how these Girl Scouts got their friends to do what they're good at!

What kind of talents are in your circle of pals?

AFTER SCHOOL, IT'S A WHIRLWIND OF PLANNING!

We'd like to *invite* you to be *part* of a community *effort*—

and have a lot of *fun* doing it!

Remember you said if I *ever* wanted to *try* building something you'd *help*?

Hello, Acme Pet?

I'm calling on behalf of the *Official* Super-ShelterMakers Committee.

Hey, Uncle Bob?

Hello, TV-10?

Have *we* got a *story* for you!

First of all, the *people* of *Glenville* owe our *thanks* to Arden Lang for *finding* these very unusual girls to help solve the problem of our under-supported shelter.

And we would like to *present* Ms. Lang with this *plaque*.

Your *honor*, I *didn't find* these Girl Scouts.

They found *me*.

And, with all due respect, *they* should *get* the plaque.

Well, girls, what do you have to *say* for yourselves?

Um...

It was *just* a matter of... of...

Of... of...

MEGAN BLURTS OUT THE WHOLE STORY, WITHOUT CALCULATING OR MEASURING A THING!

We *found* a box of *puppies*, took them to the *shelter*, found Arden Lang *exhausted*, and decided that there was a *whole* lot more to do than *just* give the pups to *her* and walk away.

Three cheers!

Girls!

Dazzle them!

I applaud girls who can mobilize the masses!

So, do you think you would have rocked the way they did if you were in their shoes?

READING
BETWEEN THE LINES

You saw how the girls in "SuperShelterMakers" took one small situation and turned it into a giant, long-lasting solution. So many decisions and actions and people went into making their project a success story!

Here's how those SuperShelterMaker girls wove their wonder web, thread by thread:

1. They found a situation they cared about.

   "Or it found them—in a box!"

2. They took immediate action to fix that problem.

   "Who wouldn't bring a box of adorable puppies home?"

3. They took a step back and looked at the big picture, asking: Is there actually a bigger problem here?

"In this case, one thing led to another. But that's sometimes how you learn the bigger picture!"

4. They looked at how the problem was related to the community. They asked: Is this an issue that the community needs to fix? How can we help?

"Sometimes realizing there's a lot more to your world takes more than you might think!"

"It might take having the nerve to speak up to adults!"
"And somehow getting them to listen to you!"

5. They brought up the issue with the community. They said, here's a problem—now, how can we fix it? They listened to what the community said, and to the people closest to the issue!

"Sometimes the best way to get people to listen to you is to LISTEN TO THEM."

6. They teamed up with each other and with the community to fix the situation.

"And everyone was happy—even the puppies!"
"The girls never forgot why they got involved in the first place."

The Good of Service and the Power of Action

Being of service to others means being helpful—doing the right and kind thing. That means feeding the hungry, clothing the homeless, or simply helping a friend with a tough homework assignment. When you serve, you answer the most basic needs: food, clothing, shelter, care.

When you move beyond immediate service to understand the cause of a problem, you move toward action. When you team up and get other people involved in your effort to solve that problem, you are taking action. Action can happen in many ways—from fixing up an animal shelter to creating a center where children who need tutoring can always get it.

Service makes the world better for some people "right now." Taking action makes the world better for more people for a much longer time. Sometimes service and action blend together into one long-lasting effort. Together, through service and action, you live the Girl Scout Law and "make the world a better place."

When you help or serve, you fulfill an immediate need. That's a good thing. But when you stretch your legs and weave your web out beyond your own circle—to create long-lasting change—you're becoming an agent of change. That's powerful!

Think About It!

Who did the "SuperShelterMakers" girls meet along the way to aid in their project?

Why was reaching out beyond their own circle important?

How is what the girls do in the story different from everyday helping out or from a basic kind of service project?

How did all the story's different characters show the Power of One?

How did the girls show the Power of Team?

FLIP THE SCRIPT

Get with your team and make your own story together. Make it a comic, a TV script, a skit—whatever helps you tell a story about girls changing the world!

(Stuck on how to start? Begin with "SuperShelterMakers" and go from there. What might happen next?)

Here are some ideas to think about:

1. What makes your heroine a good character for a supergirl?

2. What obstacle(s) does she have to overcome?

3. How does she use her power in innovative ways to solve her problem(s)?

4. Where does your heroine get her real "power"—from her superpower or from within?

Now, just go ahead and make the story your own!

Get inspired!
Get artsy with it!
Is your story on a giant roll of paper?
On cardboard strung together?
Show it off!
Who can you tell it to? Younger girls?

This activity is part of earning the Power of Team Award! Be on a team to rewrite "SuperShelterMakers" into a TV script—or make up your own supergirl comic-book story.

The Power of Community

A fish tank is a community *(with a "school" of fish!)*.

A school is a community. *(Hey! Study that idea!)*

A soccer team is a community. *(score!)*

A temple *(or church or synagogue)* is a community.

A lunchroom is a community *(at lunchtime!)*.

A table of friends in a lunchroom is a community.
(We always sit here, trading stories and sandwiches.)

The Internet is a community *(just huuuge)*.

A chat room is a community *(lol)*.

A city is a community *(24-7)*.

A chess club is a community. *(It's your move.)*

Why not aim big? Those girls with the pups got their whole town involved. Me? I'm weaving together my best web team and then we're headed toward a better world for spiders!

Mapping Communities

DEZ'S MAP

SPIDER DRAMA CLUB

SPIDER SCHOOL

SPIDER SCHOOL

SPIDERS

SPIDER SPORTS

GO!

SPIDER FOOD COURT

SPIDER MALL

SPIDER HOME

SPIDER MALL

SPIDER MALL

SPIDER MALL

SPIDER LIBRARY

YOUR MAP

How many communities are you a part of? Think about all the communities you belong to. Write them down. Then create your own crazy map of your communities that shows you at the intersection of them all.

Now, get together with your friends and make a mega-map showing ALL your communities!

Change It Up!

ANIMALS

"As in four legs, wild or tame or otherwise, at home, in the zoo, in the woods, in the sky!"

EDUCATION

"As in reading, writing, and 'rithmetic!"

(Hint: What do younger kids need?)

ENVIRONMENT

"As in trees, grass, the sea, the air or lack thereof!"

(Hint: How could you care for the natural world around you?)

FRIENDSHIP

"Who might really need some friendship?"

GOOD HEALTH

"As in gotta keep active to keep healthy. And we gotta eat right."

HOMELESSNESS

"I know we can't build a whole house, but . . . can we start somewhere?"

LITERACY

"There are grownups who never got the chance to learn to read!"

VOTING

"Sometimes people don't get to exercise their own constitutional right to cast a vote. Find out why. Cast your vote for voting!"

SAFETY

"After school, in the community, at home, and where else?"

SENIOR CITIZENS

"Because they deserve to get as much attention as they give!"

TRANSPORTATION

"You know that intersection is so hard to cross, especially with a bike!"

GREAT IDEAS!
TAKE ACTION PROJECTS
WORTH TAPPING INTO

Sure, you want to take action, but what exactly can you do? How can you make your Take Action Project really count? Here are a few ideas.

A Food Drive with Great Taste

Have you ever peeked into the collection box for a food bank? Cans of beans, boxed cereal, canned beets and peas, tomato paste. Can you imagine a meal made of that combo? Yuck!

Most food banks work hard to provide healthy and appealing food. Some take in huge donations from food companies and restaurants. Some offer—and ask for—fresh and frozen food along with the usual canned and dry foods. So how could you and your Girl Scout team kick things up a notch the next time someone suggests you take part in a food drive? Here's an idea:

Call a food bank in your area and perhaps arrange to meet with members of the staff or volunteers. Maybe they can even visit your team. Get an idea of how the food bank operates, who it serves, what it needs, and what its clients might want. Based on what you learn, you could end up doing something like this:

Your team of Girl Scouts decides to think about some simple, nutritious, and oh, so yummy meals that are easy to make—and are exactly what the people served by the food bank want. Maybe it's whole-wheat pasta with tomato sauce (you can even break down the sauce into donated items: canned tomatoes, tomato paste, olive oil), followed by a peach-and-pineapple dessert. Once you settle on a meal (or two or three), you create a plan to collect only the needed ingredients for those meals. That means being specific about the needs of your food drive in all your posters, e-mails, and fliers—and any time you talk about what you're doing. Remember: You want to be giving the food bank what its customers want. So be clear that you are collecting only the foods on your list.

Once donations roll in, you and your team sort them into "Meal in a Bag" donations ready to go to your local food bank—or deliver them in whatever way the food bank prefers. If you take the "Meal in a Bag" route, you could even include a recipe card or two in each bag and note what fresh food, if any, is needed to complete the meal. It's possible the food bank has those fresh additions on hand to add in.

No food bank in your community?

You can offer this Take Action Project through a place of worship or a community center—or any other location that helps feed people in need.

Be a Protector!

Suppose you and your team are animal and nature lovers and you want to help the environment, too. What animal or plant needs protection in your neck of the woods? Yes, even urban areas have plants and critters that need protection. So, what's threatened in your area? What's on the nation's endangered-species list? It could be a flying squirrel or a bighorn sheep, the California condor, a whooping crane, or even a crow. It could be the Texas prairie dawn-flower or the Willamette daisy. It could even be a spider. (Don't tell Dez, but about a dozen of her kin are on the endangered list!)

So huddle up and figure out who to talk to and who to meet—park rangers, local environmental groups, Nature Conservancy members, local Sierra Club representatives. Many people in your community are likely to be knowledgeable about plants and animals that could use your help.

If you pool your moxie and do some research, you and your team can become experts on an endangered or threatened species in your area. Once you know all the facts, you could create a care kit about the best ways to protect the species and its habitat. Then make copies of your kit and distribute it—at your school, other area schools, or perhaps throughout the whole community—so everyone can work to protect what's threatened in your area. You'll have learned so much that someone may want to interview you!

If you can pull something like this off, you'll have a great story to tell. Send me a copy!

Things to Think About

There are two main ways of taking action, and they are equally important.

Up-front action

means you work personally with the people you're helping. You might:

Team up with a group of senior citizens to plan a garden and then work together to make it happen.

What else can you think of?

Who else can you involve?

Behind-the-scenes action

means you work indirectly with the people you are helping by collecting resources to benefit them or finding creative ways to educate, inspire, or advocate for others on an issue. You might:

Spark the imagination of little kids who need help learning to read by joining with them to create stories.

What else can you think of?

Who else can you involve?

Can you see how you might weave together up-front action and behind-the-scenes action for a superpowerful project?

READY, SET, ACTION!

Wanted

Girl Scout Juniors who want to take action to make their community better.

Pay: New knowledge, skills, faith in yourself, fun, new friends, loads of gratitude!

Schedule: Now (and maybe later, too)!

Location: Your brain, notebooks, friends' houses, meeting places, your kitchen table, wherever you set up your project—the community, the whole world!

Participation automatically endows individual with a MOXIE WITH HONORS degree!

A great Take Action Project has many steps. But when you break them down, one by one, a project can move ahead smoothly.

Weave Your Way to a Great Take Action Project

3. Create Your Action Plan

1. Choose Your Project

4. Do the Project

2. Write Your Team Decision/Team Hopes

5. Reflect and Celebrate!

To earn your **Power of Team Award**, you have a few last things to do. Team up with your friends and choose a project that excites you all. Then write your Team Decision/Team Hopes. This also sets you up in great shape for your Take Action Project.

TEAM DECISION/TEAM HOPES

Our team decision for the Take Action Project is:

Our hopes are to:

Talk to some people like _____

Make a difference by _____

Learn more about _____

Get more people to _____

We also hope to:

Moxie up the
team

Congratulations!

You've earned your Power of Team Award! Live it up!

CREATE YOUR ACTION PLAN

✓ 1. Choose Your Project

✓ 2. Write Your Team Decision/Team Hopes

3. Create Your Action Plan

4. Do the Project

5. Reflect and Celebrate!

You know what you want to do—and you know you can do it. How are you going to make it happen?

First, research your project issue to understand:

- What the problem is

- Why it happened

- Who it affects

- How it affects them

- What you want to do to help

- What you can expect to accomplish with your project

Next, figure out what **resources** you have to draw from. Knowing your resources will help you set realistic **goals** for what you can accomplish.

Here's a breakdown. Add and delete according to your needs and your project.

PEOPLE RESOURCES
Cooperation, Communication, and Contacts

- People already involved in your issue whom you can work with

- People who care about the issue and want to help

- People with skills, such as PR or outreach, who can help you develop your skills

- Phone numbers of local media to publicize the issue

"STUFF" RESOURCES
Supplies and More

- Phones

- Notebooks and pens

- E-mail and Internet access

- Art materials for posters and publicity

"REALITY" CHECK
(as in, But There're Only, Um, 5 of Us!)

- Amount of girl power on your team

- Time you have to spend on your project

- Access to resources

- Access to the place where the issue is located

- Transportation (keep it safe!)

Everybody Loves PIE!

Need to visualize your resources? Try this with your friends:

- Divide up the pie above to review your available resources.
- Put your known resources into their proper sections of the pie.
- What slices of the pie is your group missing?

Mobilize the globe

Tapping into Resources Outside Your Group

- Who has power to give you what you want?
- What strengths can they offer your project, including financial or expert advice and support?
- How can you get their commitment to help?

WHO'S GOING TO DO WHAT?
ORGANIZING YOUR PROJECT TEAMS

Think of a racing sailboat. With the right crew and the right conditions, it can speed ahead with the wind. But everyone has a job to do. And if one person slacks off, the whole boat slows down.

Everyone has different strengths and passions. What are yours? Take a look at your project as a bunch of steps or to-do's. Which do you want to tackle?

Remember: You can also break the project down into project teams. Then each team breaks down all the steps involved in its job. So each team knows its where, when, what, and how. Moxie up those management skills! Customize your logistics! Think micro and achieve megamaxi results!

Here are some possible to-do's:

- Make a budget. (Head to the discount store!)

- Arrange transportation to and from the project site.

- Do advance publicity. (Call the media, create and post fliers: NEWSFLASH! The End-Global-Warming—One Person at a Time in This Town—Project starts Wednesday!)

- Prepare the site (with tables, decorations, special notices, permissions, restroom directions, refreshments, places to sit, places to mingle, bells to jingle).

- Recruit family members to pitch in. (Um, Mom? Grandpa? You know how you have that vacation planned...?)

- Communicate with the organization you're working with (Hello, Central? This is Ms. TOTALLY IN CONTROL).

- Set up a phone tree for project day to get the word out. (I call two friends, they call two friends, and then they call two friends...)

- Arrange for the school paper to cover the event. (Hey, Ace, have I got news for you!)

- Write a story about it! (A Major Good Deed and Funfest Happened Here in Toledo)

CHART IT OUT

Now put all your planning together on paper. Fill in this handy chart:

Project Task	Who's Doing It	Reaching Out: Who in the Community Will Be Involved?	Supplies Needed	Date Task Is to Be Finished

Think About It!

What do you like most about your plan? Why?

Now put your project in motion and you'll earn the **Power of Community Award!**

COMMUNITY

SPICE UP YOUR PROJECT

Slogans and Songs

Think up a great slogan for your project. Doing recycling? How about: Smashing! (for can crushing to save space) or Foiled Again! (for collecting used aluminum foil).

What are some great songs to play on your project days?

Don't Forget to Take Five

Make like game day, when coaches "take five" to huddle with their teams to make sure everyone knows what to do. Take five and check how everyone on your team is doing. A huddle is good for staying upbeat.

Reflection and Celebration

Once the Take Action Project is done, it's important to "debrief" and talk about the experience with your whole team. Think about:

- Your hopes for the project. What did you want to accomplish? Did you achieve it all?
- The steps. How did each one go?
- Your goal. Did you meet it? Did it change?
- Your teamwork. How'd you do together?
- Compare your project to the one in the "SuperShelterMakers" story. Did you and the girls in the story follow through on all the Take Action steps?

Decide together how and when you want to celebrate this leadership journey.

Plan big, because you made the journey from...

Power of One to Power of Team to Power of Community and from...

Being Girl Scout Juniors to becoming

Agents of change!

Ideas for the Big Celebration

Hang a poster-size copy of your project chart in your gathering space and then:

SET ASIDE SOME TIME FOR REFLECTION.

If you could keep your project going, what would you continue? What would you change?

WRITE A COMMUNITY PROCLAMATION.

Write a proclamation to continue your commitment to the community. Frame it and present it to the organizers you teamed with.

CLAP YOUR HANDS AND SAY THANKS.

Each person gets a chance to stand up and say who she thanks for assisting her with this Take Action Project. After each name, clap your hands and say, "Yeah!" Make it as exciting and loud as you can! Make it a massive cheer! End, if you feel like it, with a mutual back patting and a friendship squeeze.

MAKE A PROJECT DAY SCRAPBOOK.

It's great to keep a record of all you've accomplished. Collect all your memories, photos, notes, and souvenirs in a project scrapbook. Then get together as a group and self-publish the book. Present it to each other, to your adult volunteer, and all the great people you partnered with.

AND NOW, A LITTLE CIRCLING BACK

Turn back to a page from the beginning of this journey and put a "before" and "after" thought into it. See how much you've learned—about leading from the inside out! You started with your own power, the Power of One, moved on to the Power of Team, and ended up with full-force Power of Community!

That makes you an Agent of Change.

Take a look at what you did to earn this title:

• You found out what was important and you found out the facts.
• You figured out the steps to accomplish your action.
• You acted as a team of leaders.
• You got together with people in your community and acted with them to create a really good change.

You got your power going just like I weave my web—from the inside out! Way to go!

Congratulate yourselves for your accomplishments as leaders and agents of change! So, what's your next project?

Your Journey, Your Memories

Wow, pages all set for a comic-book story! I'm gonna weave a new power tale here—with all *my* favorite parts of this power-filled journey. How about *you*?